MAKE MONEY FROM HOME

I0037392

A Step-by-Step Guide to make money from home with work from home jobs

BOOK DESCRIPTION

Work-from-home jobs have been on a steady increase over time. This has been due to the internet revolution that has brought about better and cheaper technologies that have made it possible to have virtual offices. Workers are able to work remotely from home or wherever they do feel at home.

This book aims to provide you with great information as a potential work-from-home employee. It also provides a glimpse to work-from-home employers about the immense benefits that they can gain from using it.

For both remote workers and employers, the book demonstrates the benefits that each gets and sheds more light on the kind of jobs that are better done remotely, and more so, from home. The book goes further to advise the would-be home-workers on how to find work-from-home jobs.

Definitely, despite professional training, each work environment requires a set of unique skills. A work-from-home environment is not an exception. This guide provides you with information on the skills you need to succeed as a remote worker.

Building an online portfolio and networking online are great ways to prepare yourself to find those well-paying work-from-home jobs. This book teaches you how to build your online portfolio and network online to be able to fish out more work opportunities.

At the end, you desire to have paid clients for you to be able to finance your lifestyle. This book guides you on how to get your first paid clients. Much more importantly, you would spend less time and effort maintaining your clients than easily losing them and keep on looking for others. In this book, you are guided on how to maintain long-term, productive and sustainable relationships with your clients.

Enjoy reading!

ABOUT THE AUTHOR

George Pain is an entrepreneur, author and business consultant. He specializes in setting up online businesses from scratch, investment income strategies and global mobility solutions. He has successfully built several businesses from the ground up and is excited to share his knowledge with you.

DISCLAIMER

Copyright © 2017

All Rights Reserved

No part of this book can be transmitted or reproduced in any form including print, electronic, photocopying, scanning, mechanical or recording without prior written permission from the author.

While the author has taken the utmost effort to ensure the accuracy of the written content, all readers are advised to follow information mentioned herein at their own risk. The author cannot be held responsible for any personal or commercial damage caused by information. All readers are encouraged to seek professional advice when needed.

CONTENTS

BOOK DESCRIPTION...2

ABOUT THE AUTHOR 4

DISCLAIMER 5

CONTENTS..6

INTRODUCTION 7

BENEFITS OF WORKING FROM HOME...................................9

TYPES OF WORK FROM HOME JOBS 23

FINDING WORK FROM HOME OPPORTUNITIES 26

WHAT SKILLS SHOULD I LEARN AND USE? 31

BUILDING YOUR ONLINE PORTFOLIO.................................39

NETWORKING ONLINE...49

HOW TO GET YOUR FIRST PAID CLIENTS 54

MAINTAINING RELATIONSHIPS WITH YOUR CLIENTS 64

CONCLUSION 79

INTRODUCTION

Work-from-home jobs have been growing at a rapid pace in the recent past. This has been due to employers realizing the win-win great benefits for them and their employees brought about by work-from-home arrangement.

There are many people out there struggling to find convenient jobs that would enable them to work while still have time at home. Some have quit working due to the attention they need to give to their loved ones at home. Others have found that the cost of commuting to work is prohibitively high and inconveniencing such that it makes no sense to continue commuting. Lack of adequate information on how to find work-from-home jobs, successfully do them and make gainful reward from them has been a great hindrance.

This book aims to provide you with helpful information about work-from-home jobs so that you can reap from their immense benefits. You will learn about the type of work-from-home jobs that you can engage in, how to find them and the kind of skills you ought to develop in order to succeed. Furthermore, you will also learn how to market yourself by building your online portfolio and networking online. Having your first paid client is a breakthrough. Maintaining productive relationships with them so that you spend less on marketing and more on working is a much bigger breakthrough. In this book, you will learn how to achieve those breakthroughs that will enable you to scale to greater heights of a rewarding work-from-home career.

Keep reading!

BENEFITS OF WORKING FROM HOME

Working from home is increasingly becoming a norm rather than an exception. More employees are choosing to work from home. A good number of employers are getting accustomed to this. Both the employees and their employers have discovered the great benefits that come with working from home.

Insights from the following info statistics will help you have a glimpse of the current state and likely future in terms of benefits of working from home.

Info Statistics

According to Global Workplace Analytics, telecommuting (work-from-home/remote working) has grown by about 80% in the period from 2005 to 2012. State governments lead in this growth by 122% followed by non-profits at 87%, for-profits by 70% and local government by 62%. This is a phenomenal increase.

A Stanford study, dubbed as 'More Productivity' discovered that work-from-home employees are 13% more productive than their counterparts working in-office are. This is what has inspired more reluctant employers to cede ground in favor of a work-from-home arrangement. This is supported by further statistics from Canada Life survey which indicate that home workers rank their productivity at 7.7/10 score compared to in-office workers who rank their productivity at 6.5/10. Canada Life also found out that home workers took an average 1.8 sick days in a year compared to in-office workers who took 3.1 days. This probably indicates that home workers are not only more productive but also healthier than their in-office counterparts.

In a recent study conducted by Brandman University, 135 key managers surveyed in companies with over 500 employees, it found out that 40% of them already use work-from-home employees extensively and 56% of them plan to increase their use. Thus, the future of work-from-home opportunities is bright.

Benefits to employee

A recent survey conducted by a reputable Human Resource firm found that:

- Sixty percent of employees prefer working from home due to the work/home balance.
- Fifty-five percent of employees preferred work from home due to saving on gas.
- Forty-seven percent of employees find work from home the most effective way of avoiding traffic.

- Forty-five percent of employees found it more productive to work from home than from office.
- Forty-four percent of employees found it less distracting while working from home.
- Forty-four percent preferred working from home as the best way to eliminate long commute.
- Forty-three percent found working from home provided a quieter environment than working from office.
- Thirty-eight percent experienced less stress working from home than from office.
- Twenty-nine percent preferred working from home as this enabled them to have more time with the family.
- Twenty-three percent found it environmentally friendly working from home than at office.

Apart from these survey findings, the following are the overall general benefits of working from home:

- You can design your office to your personal liking. Unlike your employer's premises, in your own premises, you can design where you work from in your own liking. Should you choose to sit on a couch or high-standing stool, it is all up to you.

- You can locate your office anywhere – Working from home means working remotely. This grants you the flexibility you need. You can work from your kitchen while using your kitchen breakfast bar as your office station. You can use your balcony as an office space. You can use your living room. You can also use a hotel room or coffee corner - just to have a change of environment. If you are tired of working indoors, you can still get to work outdoors - your backyard garden, by the beachside, or even in a park! All these are flexible options available to you that you will not find in your office.

- Real money saving – Other than saving on commuting charges, you can save on the cost you would incur on buying lunch, polishing your shoes, special office wardrobe, etc.

- Flexible time schedule – Not all of us work optimally during the normal office schedule. There are those who find themselves at their optimal working as from 4:00 am. Some others find themselves optimal working from 10:00 am. Yet still, there are those rare creative minds (especially programmers, software developers, artists, etc) that find their creative minds optimized at wee hours of the night. If your employer does not care about your work schedule but results, then, you are as free as a flying bird to work from home.

- Time-saving – There is plenty of time wasted on commuting. This time can be saved towards work. Even if not work, you can utilize your saving towards rest, leisure or even extra sleep! These help to boost your immune system, health, and mental acuity.
- Healthy eating – Most of us find it hard to carry packed lunch. We find it convenient to eat at a hotel or fast food joint. The unfortunate thing is that you have no control over the ingredients of hotel food. Thus, you cannot observe diet. You cannot keep off bad cholesterol foods. You cannot have it fresh. These eventually eat up your medical bills and lower your productivity. While at home, you can eat your desired healthy food at your own convenience. Eventually, you become healthier, less stressed (by avoiding oxidative food-oriented stress).
- Wage optimization – Working from home allows you a chance to work with different employers. This helps you to not only optimize your earning potential but also reduce the risk of redundancy occasioned by being sacked and spending time looking for another job. Yes, you can employ diversification to cut down on the risk of unemployment.

- You can work as you learn – The challenges of modernity are that you need to keep on acquiring new skills to remain relevant in the marketplace. While working at the office, chances of taking part-time studies in-between your work schedule become difficult. With your own work schedule, you can easily pop-in to learn a few things online while taking a break from work. Yet still, most work-from-home jobs are research-intensive. This, by their very own nature, allows you to keep on acquiring new skills thus boosting your own potential for better-paying jobs.

- More enjoyable and effective meetings – While at the office, there is that strain and stress of organizing and/or attending meetings. While at home, you can easily organize online meet-ups. You can easily have teleconferences. You can attend webinars. Much more, you can easily and cheaply record meetings for your future references.

- You can keep in touch more easily and effectively – Working from home not only enables you to easily get in touch with colleagues online, especially if they are also working online, but you can also easily meet with those within your locality. There are many chatting tools with fun effects such as emojis, chat room 'bots', virtual top hat (Hangouts), and great anniversary celebrations cards, GIFs and other animations which helps to boost interactions. This, you can do at any time. Keeping in touch online is more effective as you can easily get straight to the point, have records of conversations kept for further reference and easily have convenient intervals without overly inconveniencing other functions such as attending to customers.

- You can stay more focused – Working from home can help you to become more disciplined. You can easily control your time between work, watching TV, playing video games and other activities. It is hard to control these in the evenings or weekends if your work from the office. However, working from home, every hour can be used for work. This mentally helps you to avoid unnecessary activities while keeping genuine rest and leisure activities intact.

- You can keep off office politics – Many careers are ruined because of office politics. A lot of health is adversely affected by the stress occasioned by office politics. Strains of meeting up to the expectations of others can also bring up stress in the office environment. While working from home, you are able to avoid office politics and its negative consequences.

- Healthy lifestyle – Apart from eating healthy, there are other health benefits of working from home. While working from home, you can easily avoid sedentary lifestyle – a disease that afflicts many office workers. At home, you can easily take small breaks to make coffee, set up lunch, tend to the garden, take your pet for a walk, go swimming, go for a 45-minute session at the gym, among such other short activities. You do not easily get strained, as you do not have to stay glued to the computer screen for long hours continuously. Furthermore, all these activities can easily utilize the time you would have wasted while commuting to and from work.
- Job satisfaction – Those who are entrusted with freedom and flexibility of working from home feel empowered. This brings more satisfaction and enthusiasm towards company's goals.

Benefits to employer

It is not just work-from-home employees who are benefiting, employers too are reaping great benefits from the work-from-home arrangement.

The following are some of the benefits employers are gaining from hiring work-from-home employees:

- Less time wastage – Less time is wasted towards commuting and even preparing to go to work.
- More productivity- A Stanford study found out that those employees who work from home are 13% more productive than their in-office counterparts are.
- More motivation - Work-life balance makes employees feel happier, more motivated and inspired to continue working. This results in higher morale, which triggers higher productivity.
- Much easier connection – With work-from-home, it is easier to connect with other employees.
- Free overtime – Work-from-home employees are more open to being engaged beyond the traditional office hours.
- Less overhead costs – You do not have to pay for office space, office facilities such as workstations, office snacks, and such other costs. Furthermore, you spend less on stationery as you would if they were working from in-office. You also save on power bills and sanitary costs.
- Fewer meetings – With work-from-home, the connection is through the internet. Due to the instant chatting facility, which allows group chats, less is spent on holding meetings. With facilities such as Skype, GoToMeeting and

others, fewer meetings are necessary, yet more quality engagements are possible.

- Qualified staff – Work-from-home provides an opportunity to hire across the globe. This opens one to an immense pool of qualified staff.

- Affordable 24/7 arrangement – With work-from-home jobs you are not restricted to traditional office hours. There are no lunch breaks or evening breaks and such like. You do not have to spend huge overtime costs of having the staff to work overnight. You simply take advantage of time zones. This way, you can have some employees working during the daytime while others are enjoying their night sleep elsewhere. You can have some working during the morning while others are enjoying their lunchtime. There is absolutely no extra cost of working all-round-the-clock.

- Less employee turnover rate – What increases the chance of employees quitting jobs is office monotony and at times conflicts between employees at work. This is minimized when working from home. Thus, employees are more likely to stay longer on a job while working from home than otherwise. If they are bored with their house environment, they can switch to another environment. Employees become more loyal to the company when granted an opportunity to work from home. With less employee turnover rate, you save on the cost of advertising for a vacancy, hiring new staff and training them to be on par with those who have exited. Furthermore, you lose productivity while they are picking up.

- Managing teams is much easier online – With facilities such as Basecamp and Asana, it is much easier to manage teams online than you would manage them offline. They have more intuitive engagement metrics, time utilization metrics, incisive records, among other features that make one easily optimize on teams.

- Multicultural market insights – With employees spread all over the world, it is easier to enrich your work environment with diversity and thus tap into positive cultural aspects to improve performance. Furthermore, you can get better market insights from employees residing in a particular market than relying on the news.

- Fewer health costs – It is common knowledge that most employees take sick leave just to have a break from work. This is less likely to occur when they are working from home. On the other hand, chances of illness spreading from one employee to another in big offices are common. With distributed workplace, those chances decrease.

Colds, flues, and such other communicable diseases will not have a great impact. Chances of food poisoning affecting a significant portion of your staff become rare.

- Fewer vacation costs – While working from home, employees are less inclined to feel the urge to go on vacation. This is not so the case with in-office workers who easily get burned-out.

- Higher output – On average, home-based employees work for longer hours compared to those who work in-office. This is because their work becomes part of their normal home activity, which they can do any time including evenings and nights. This is not so the case with in-office workers who have to abide by the normal work shift schedule.

- Positive environmental impact – Working from home reduces carbon emissions due to commuting. It also reduces paperwork. Reduced paperwork means less forest is destroyed. With fewer forests destroyed, more trees are available to sweep the atmosphere off carbons.

- Work with friends – Certain non-sensitive work can easily be done with friends. For example, creative design work, software development, etc can easily be enhanced by working with friends. Thus, the employer gets the extra benefit of receiving input from those not hired for the job.

- Good for employees with disability – It is expensive to have the right facility for employees with disability in an office environment and even in the commuter system. Yet, it is quite inconveniencing for them to commute daily to work. Work from home enables employees with a disability to contribute from the comfort of their environment while the employer benefits from their skills without incurring extra costs.

Employer concerns

The greatest concern for those employers who are reluctant to hire work-from-home employees is the loss of control over their staff when they choose to work from home. However, these concerns can be easily addressed by a change in attitude and re-organization on the way work is done.

The following are some of the ways employers can address these concerns:

- Quantify work and thus make it measurable
- Schedule work
- Have elaborate reporting system
- Measure performance in term of results

- Make reward to be based on results rather than activity

As a potential work-from-home jobseeker, these are the concerns that you have to address as you persuade your employer to consider work-from-home as the best arrangement for you. Your success in convincing your current or potential employer means your freedom to work from home.

TYPES OF WORK FROM HOME JOBS

As more employers come to appreciate work-from-home arrangements, different types of work are becoming available. Employers who have enjoyed the benefits that come with working from home have created unique opportunities by simply repackaging their office work to become doable at home.

The following are the main types of work at home jobs:

- Data entry – e.g. data entry clerks
- Telesales and marketing jobs – e.g. sales representative, account executive/manager, marketing manager
- Professional services and consultancy jobs – e.g. Human Resources administration, accountancy, bookkeeping, etc
- Customer service – e.g. customer service representative, call center operator
- Virtual assistance
- Writing, editing, translation, and research – e.g. magazine writer, content writer, journalism, copywriters, bloggers, ghostwriter, author, etc.
- Engineering design

- Software development
- Web design & Development – web designer, web tester, etc
- UI/UX Design
- Systems Analysts
- Travel counselors
- Medical Coder
- Case manager
- Bilingual interpreter
- Project/program manager
- Graphic designer
- Insurance adjuster
- SEO expert (e.g. for Search Engine Advertising)
- Business development manager
- Education consultants - e.g. Online Tutors/instructors/lecturers,
- Language teaching and translation - language teachers, language evaluators, virtual tutors, etc
- Technical support providers
- Search Engine Evaluator
- Transcription – e.g. transcribers
- Surveys – e.g. survey taker
- Website tester, software tester, etc
- Video filming and posting – e.g. 'How-to', DIY, videos

- Social Media Marketing
- Blogging
- Affiliate marketing
- Sports Betting & Arbitrage Trading
- E-commerce
- Online Casino

FINDING WORK FROM HOME OPPORTUNITIES

Many people out there are enjoying fulfilling careers working from home. Maybe you are probably wondering where to start.

The following are some of the ways by which you can start searching for work from home jobs:

1. Use existing freelancing sites

If you were a beginner, you probably would like to start from the tested and proven sources. Freelancing sites are tested and proven. However, most of them offer very low paying jobs. Maybe, it could be a place to start and then scale-up as you gain experience and exposure.

The following are popular freelancing sites that you can try:

General freelancing sites:

- Upwork.com
- Freelancer.com
- Fiverr.com

Web design, coding, and programming sites:

- Treehouse.com

2. Use job boards and job listing sites

Job listing sites are some kind of aggregation sites listing jobs from across the world. The following are the popular job listing sites:

- Jobrapido.com
- Craiglist.com
- LinkUp.com
- SimplyHired.com
- Indeed.com
- Flexijobs.com
- Popular job boards include; CareerBuilder, Monster, Dice, LinkedIn etc.

Academic writing jobs:

These are sites that offer student assistance jobs. You can help students write term papers, research papers, thesis, etc.

- Uvocorp.com
- Researchwritingcenter.com

3. Use your network

Get in touch with your alumni association and former colleagues to let them know that you are seeking work-from-home jobs.

4. Use social media

Social media sites and groups have places where you can find jobs. LinkedIn is a professional site for employers and job seekers. Create a profile, specifically tailor it to work-from-home jobs, market your skills and interact with others. You could get an employer interested in your skills and mode of working. Facebook has groups focused on work-at-home jobs. Find some of these groups and join them.

5. Focus on specific companies

There are certain specific companies that are already providing work-from-home opportunities for certain jobs. List them and follow-up on them so that you are able to detect when there is an opening. Talking to them too can help, even if there is no vacancy now. Some may still have openings for part-time or stand-in employee when their regular employee is sick, on maternity leave or annual leave. Furthermore, some jobs may have peak season when they require temporary staff to help. You can begin this way as you gain their confidence towards full-time.

6. Ask your boss

If you are already working in an office, you may ask your boss about the possibility of working from home. He probably could be thinking the same but wondering how you would react to it. On the other hand, your boss could probably not be aware that your kind of job could be done from home. What you need is to inform your boss of the benefits the company would derive from you working from home. In addition, you will need to prove how you can maintain the same level of productivity, if not higher. Take initiative and prove ways and means by which you can achieve these. If possible, request for a few days a week for a work-from-home experiment. It could be one day a week or twice a week.

Be wary of frauds

There are many job seekers out there. Some of them are desperate enough to be conned. Be cautious while seeking jobs online. The following are some of the telling signs that you are most likely dealing with a scammer:

- Being asked to pay in order to get a job
- Being promised a pay that is just too good to be true

How to avoid online job fraud:

- Avoid paying in order to get a job
- Research on the company - Several sites exists to help you flag out scammers. If you find a company or website offering a job, simply type its name into the search engine bar and add the word "legit?" and click to search. Known scammers will appear on many anti-scam sites. You will be able to read from testimonies of those who have been scammed. However, use prudence since there are some disgruntled employees who can choose to spoil the name of an employer. Some competitors may also do that. The secret is, read from as many anti-scamming sites as possible. If a site is cited by several anti-scamming sites, keep off from it.
- Keep-off get-rich-quick schemes – Those sites that promise huge salaries, fewer working hours and the like are too good to be true. Most of them are scammers who will eventually find ways to defraud you.
- No skill required – Most jobs require you to have a specific set of skills. Any advert that tells you that there is no skill required and "anyone can do" yet offer hefty wages are most likely going to be swindling sites.

WHAT SKILLS SHOULD I LEARN AND USE?

Working from home requires more skills than you would ordinarily require while working at the office. This is more so if you are working as an independent freelancer who has to deal with several employers at a time and each time has to send proposals and bids for jobs.

The following are typical skills you would require to have a successful work from home career:

1. Communication skills
2. Technical skills
3. Professional skills
4. Marketing skills
5. Interpersonal relationship skills
6. Leadership skills

Communication skills

You should be able to have excellent written and verbal communication skills. You should be able to interact with your clients and colleagues in various communication platforms such as Skype, Whatsapp, Facebook Messenger, chat tools, among others. You should be able to engage them effectively in video conference meetings, webinars, etc. In addition, you should be able to have a great listening ability so that you can be able to not only listen to what someone is saying but also what someone is trying hard not to say.

Technical skills

Technical skills depend on the kind of job that you are looking for. However, we can classify these skills into two main categories:

- Broad general skills
- Specific technical skills

Broad skills are the general skills that virtually anyone working online should possess. These include:

- Typing skills – You should be able to type fast enough. This is not only good for writing assignments but also chat communication
- Communication skills – You should not only prove oral and written communication but also ability to use common communication tools such as email, Skype, Hangout, Whatsapp, Telegram, and other chatting and

calling tools. You should also be able to have excellent telephone etiquette.

- Remote team-working skills – You should be able to work with other remote workers as a team.
- Time consciousness – Working remotely means that you could be working with people from different time zones. This means that when you are scheduling meeting appointments, you be conscious of this and be able to specify the time zone of the meeting time. For example, if you are in San Francisco and your workmate or company is in New York, you can say, "Let's meet online on Thursday, December 21, at 11 AM Pacific Time (San Francisco) / 2 PM Eastern Time (NYC)." Other than time zones, it is important to keep time.
- Self-discipline
- Result-oriented
- Professionalism
- Flexible and adaptable – In remote work-from-home, you are more likely going to encounter with colleagues and clients across the globe. They will be people from diverse cultures and different work ethics. Thus, you should be

flexible enough to deal with them and more adaptable to their specific requirements.

- Self-initiative and resourcefulness – Working from home require self-initiative. You do not have to wait to be prompted to do what you ought to do. Most of the challenges you will encounter will require your own initiative to find solutions. Taking an extra step and showing your employer that you are ready for the task helps to build confidence in your abilities.

Specific technical skills are those skills that are uniquely particular to the kind of job you are seeking. The following are some of the common specific technical skills:

- Copywriting
- Marketing
- Coding
- Tech-savvy – Have some basic hardware and software skills. This could include software installation, hardware maintenance, networking, tethering, etc.

Professional skills

Professional skills fall into two broad categories:

- Trained professional skills
- Consultancy skills

Trained professional skills are those professional skills that you acquire through formal training, either at the college level or at the university level. Most professionals fall into this category. These include lawyers, accountants, engineers, doctors, among others.

Consultancy skills are acquired through practice and experience. They could be advanced with technical or professional skills. They are unique in their own regard as they relate to a specific niche. They are usually a blend of various forms of technical and professional skills. For example, online business consultancy, SEO consultancy, etc.

Marketing skills

Marketing is not only a professional skill but also a skill required by most work-from-home jobs. This is more so when you are a freelance work-from-home employee. As a freelance worker, you are more often than not, going to market yourself to get jobs from various employers. This becomes of paramount importance.

Leadership skills

These skills are required for one to be able to lead others. They are not isolated from but an addition to general skills, technical skills, professional skills and marketing skills. This leadership could be personnel leadership, thought leadership or a combination of both. When you are a remote worker, you will hardly rely on others to lead you. You are largely your own boss. Thus, unlike in-office workers, leadership skills are critical to your own success as a remote work-from-home worker. The following are some of the leadership skills you would require:

- Organization – You should be able to be self-organized and by that extension be able to organize others. In organizing, you should be able to match people and resources in such a manner that optimizes their output at the least cost possible.
- Motivation – You need the ability not only to motivate yourself but others. Probably a few out there will find remote working less motivating and thus would need a boost of morale from you.
- Self-sufficiency – You not only need to be self-reliant but also self-sufficient when working from home. In an office work environment, you can easily find a helping hand on a common task. You can even delegate or assign someone else. However, in a work-from-home environment, you are you very own helping hand. You have to acquire necessary skills and predisposition that would enable you to be your very own help.

- Communication – You should not only be able to express yourself clearly and articulately but also have great listening skills. You should be able to be the one who takes time to listen to others rather than talking to them. You should be able to tap, synthesize and digest their concerns so that you come up with effective solutions. In qualitative listening, you are able to relate to them and build rapport.
- Adept at using technology – e.g. Skype, Hangouts, Join.me, Dropbox, etc
- Critical thinking – Critical thinking requires that you not only find new solutions but also critically evaluate existing solutions to establish their reliability, validity, and efficacy. This way, you are able to find alternative ways of optimizing solutions.
- Proactive – Be able to think in advance of possible solutions for likely scenarios.
- Good planner – Planning is an important and inevitable quality of a great leader. Good planning skills are essential to being able to lead others. You should be able to utilize planning and project management tools.
- Balance – Working from home means that you have freedom. You have access to everything you would admire

while in office. You have to balance between the needs of your work and the needs for your home so that none are inadvertently sacrificed for the benefit of the other.

- Independence – You should be capable of making independent decisions related to work.
- Confidence – You should manifest a high degree of confidence in your knowledge, skills, and abilities. While you can easily gauge the mood and feelings of others in an in-office environment, the same is not the case when working remotely. Thus, confidence is critical.
- Professionalism – You have to maintain highest standards of work ethics and professionalism. Being respectful to all key stakeholders, including staff, customers, and other independent contractors is crucial. You are the voice of your company and ought to represent what it stands for in terms of its vision, mission and core values.

BUILDING YOUR ONLINE PORTFOLIO

Getting work-from-home jobs is like having a consultancy job. You have to build your portfolio not only to introduce yourself but also to highlight your skills, talents, experience, and expertise. This way, your potential clients gets to have a deeper insight of what to expect from you.

Who should set up an online job search portfolio?

If you are a professional, consultant, or independent contractor, then, having a portfolio is the best way to establish yourself as a brand, market yourself, and search for jobs.

The following are some of the professionals that take advantage of their online portfolio to pitch for jobs and contracts:

- Marketers/Advertisers
- Performers, Musicians, Actors, Artists
- Fitness and Sports professionals
- Journalists and Writers
- Translators, Professors, Teachers, Tutors
- Professional Designers

- Real Estate Professionals
- Researchers and Scientists

Even if you happen not to be in this list, or among those professionals that are not allowed to advertise for their services, you can simply put your portfolio online for informational purposes. This way, you use it during your job Applications. It can immensely reduce paperwork during your Application process.

An online portfolio is a great marketing tool. You need to have one. It is critical to your success, especially if you are working on a freelance basis.

The following are key steps to building, publishing and publicizing your online portfolio:

Step 1: Consider Your End Goals

You have to determine whether your end goal is getting a new job or you are content with your existing job (maybe as a full-time employee) and just want to brand yourself. If you are looking for a new job, you have to determine whether you are looking for a freelancing job or a full-time employee job. Your end goal will determine how you design your portfolio.

Whichever the case, your online portfolio should be about creating an online identity geared towards establishing a personal brand.

Step 2: Create a portfolio to highlight what you want others to see

The portfolio should highlight what you want others to see. It is about creating an impression for the future direction of your career. For example, you could have been working in the office as a full-time employee in a career that is hardly possible to work-from-home, for example, as an air hostess. Now you want to switch to a career that is easier to work from home, for example, travel consultant. In this case, you will focus less on your experience as Air Hostess. Instead, you will dwell more on what you aspire to do as a travel consultant.

Thus:

- Focus on creating an online impression or identity what fits your dream career.
- Emphasize on your strengths in areas that you are endearing. Emphasize on relevant education and skills that support your goal.

- Prove your knowledge and expertise by posting blogs in that area you are focused on.
- Position yourself as an expert in that field and master of your craft.

A good portfolio ought to have the following:

1. About Me/Bio

Your bio should have:

- Your photo
- Your name
- An introduction of who you are
- A powerful statement about what you do, your intents and what you can deliver
- A compelling call-to-action statement

The bio should be about yourself (your personality and optimism), your experience and your openness to future assignments.

2. Resume/Career highlights

Make a brief overview of your resume by highlight key points. This is a summary of your resume. Provide a link to the following:

- Your online Resume (in HTML format) – This allows potential clients to have a look at your resume while still online.
- Downloadable Resume (in PDF format) – This allows your potential clients to have a copy of your Resume for offline reading and filing for future reference.

If for some valid reasons that you do not want your resume to be publicly available, you can create password-protected pages such that only those who are seriously interested in you can get in touch so that you grant them the password.

Make sure that the highlights are more biased towards your accomplishments. Each highlight should have a link to work that you have done that is available on the web. For example, if you are a writer, your blog. In case, you are a web designer - your designed websites. You can also provide links to your previous employers' websites.

3. Snippets of your work (work portfolio)

This should give a glimpse of your work. It should include written pieces (for writers), published works (e.g. research publications), keynote addresses, pictures, certifications, articles/posts, podcasts, and videos, among others.

If you do not have much to highlight, endeavor to build up your body of work. The following are two ways by which you can achieve this:

- Personal projects – These are projects that you have created out of your own initiative for your own benefit and/or those you care for. These help to prove your self-drive and self-motivation. In addition, they prove your ability to work independently. These are core competencies required for work-from-home contractors.
- Pro-bono projects – These are projects that have been devised by others, but you have delivered them free of charge or just at a small stipend. Pro-bono projects are usually for charity and voluntary work for the benefit of the vulnerable and/or less fortunate members of society. If you do not have sufficient work experience, these can boost your portfolio. These are also a great source of quality referrals.

4. Recommendation Quotes

These are quotes from previous clients about how great it has been to work with you. It is always good to seek feedback or honest recommendation about work that you have successfully completed for your clients. This way, you can be able to have a rich source of recommendation quotes from them.

5. Social Network presence

The following are great social networking platforms on which you can establish your authoritative presence:

- LinkedIn – You ought to have a LinkedIn account. If you have not already, it is worth creating. This helps to make you appear more professional. Most potential employers and recruiters have LinkedIn profiles. They will feel more at ease with you if you do have a LinkedIn profile. Invite them to your LinkedIn profile.

- Twitter – Twitter is a great place for most corporate clients. This is from where they publicize their news and info to a wider audience. Having a Twitter account means that you can follow them and they too can follow you. Invite them to your Twitter handle.

- Instagram – If you are dealing with creative minds, then, Instagram is a great place to be. You can highlight your designs and follow their designs right there. Invite them too. Even if you are a writer or other professional, it is good to have Instagram to highlight your portfolio clips.

- Facebook – A good number of clients have Facebook pages. Invite them to your Facebook Page. It is good to have a Page if you have a great collection of work portfolio (avoid directing your potential clients to your personal profile as this has more personal things that may not be in line with what you would wish them to know). Positive comments from your followers can inspire your potential clients to hire you.

- YouTube Channel – If you are specialized in jobs that require video creation, this is a necessity. You can also have your portfolio in a short video. If it is well done, be sure this can work great for you. Invite them to your YouTube channel.

- Google Plus – Google has a host of products for business, more so, Google for Business. If your potential clients are the types that are more likely to have Google for Business, then, your Google Plus account is a way to show them that you are familiar with their work environment.

6. Blog

Blogging is important for all professionals, especially those working on freelance and consultancy basis. A blog helps you to demonstrate greater knowledge and expertise in your specialized field. It allows your potential clients to have a deeper insight into not only your knowledge and expertise but also passion towards your career and profession. If you do not have a blog, you had better start now. Post by post, you will find yourself having a great blog site.

This is not just for your potential clients. It also helps you to carry out further research as you write, build up your writing skills, engagement skills (by responding to comments on your blog) and consolidating your knowledge by getting rid of knowledge gaps.

A blog is also a place from where you can market your online portfolio. You simply write a blog post, give your name and provide a link to your portfolio. Other than marketing your portfolio, it is also a market in itself. You never know which potential client is reading it.

WordPress is a great blog app to use.

7. Contact Info

Never forget to give your contact info. How else will your potential employer contact you? Make sure that you leave your email, and if possible, telephone contact. If you are concerned about spam mail, create a contact form instead so that whoever wants to contact you fills details in the contact form. This way, you will receive communication without publicly disclosing your email address to spammers.

If you are regularly online, you can also provide chat facility. Providing Skype, Whatsapp or Telegram chatting facility is a greater way of clients finding you. Their messages will also reach your phone wherever you are. In fact, this is the best way to do deal with contacts.

Step 3: Market your portfolio

The first marketing strategy is to have your portfolio domain in your name. This way, potential employers searching for you can easily find you on the Search Engine list. Yes, someone may stumble upon your portfolio but forget to put down details. Remembering your name would make the person easily search for your profile. Furthermore, your name is your brand. It is what you are marketing.

Publicize your profile in your blog posts and Social media accounts by linking it to them. If you have some cash, you can even advertise your portfolio.

NETWORKING ONLINE

To succeed in whatever career that you are undertaking, there is no shortcut but to network. Networking is the social platform you need to establish your foundation for growth. It is through networking that you receive feeder channels of opportunity. You are like a fresh lake – you receive a constant flow of opportunities from others – yet to remain fresh, you also have to supply opportunities to others.

Thanks to the advent of the internet, reaching out to people across the globe is easy as knocking on your neighbor's door. Over 3 billion people are active on social media each day. If you endeavored to meet all of them, you will not even manage 1% of them before your lifespan expires. Such is the immense opportunity available on the social network.

Yet, even with such a huge population of people online, it is not necessary that you will be able to establish a productive work relationship with most people. This is why you have to confine yourself to those whom you share interests, passion and concerns.

The following are simple ways by which you, as a remote work-at-home employee can be able to network online:

1. Join LinkedIn groups

LinkedIn is by far the largest professional social networking platform in the world. Here is a place where professionals like you find a home. Here is the place where employers and recruiters visit to fish for potential employees. Here is the single-most concentration of professionals where you can easily find like-minded people – be they co-workers, partners or employers.

Since LinkedIn is such a diverse network, you can seem lost in a large forest. Thus, you need to cut out a territory reachable by you. Joining groups is the best way to do this. Find groups relevant to your interests. Request to join them. Once you are allowed to join them, be an active participant. You can ask questions, seek potential opportunities and surely, you will not miss being guided.

2. Reconnect with your alma mater

Bonds established while at college are usually strong and easy to trigger no matter how long you have been apart. Most alma mater groups have an online presence. Join them. Even if you do not find your group, create one. Get in touch with a few that you know and can reach to join the group. Share ideas. Build rapport. Introduce to them what you do as a work-at-home professional.

Request them to help you if they know of any similar opportunities.

Extol the virtues of your mode of working so that they can buy into it. Some could be decision-makers in their workplaces who can create an avenue for you.

Use co-working space

The modern physical workspace has changed. It is not rare to find independent professionals from diverse backgrounds coming together to share a common working space. This is a cheaper co-working option where people can share common resources that would otherwise be expensive to acquire and largely redundant if done by a single individual. In the co-working environment, people share common reception service, common printer, internet, common furniture e.g. office desk/table, etc. Some co-working spaces allows you to book specific days, certain hours. You can opt for a few hours a day, few days a week to work from there. This way, you can build new networks. Furthermore, there is a higher potential of getting a small assignment from co-workers.

Join organizations in your community and check out for networking events

If you happen to live in big cities, there are plenty of networks specifically formed to connect young professionals. If you do not know of any group, do a Google search for one in your locality. You could be surprised at the availability of such networks within your locality.

Even without the presence of a professional networking group within your locality, you can still join a community group to offer voluntary services during your free time. More so, voluntary services relate to your field of specialty. This way, you will not only be opening yourself up to potential future opportunities, but you will also be building up your profile. You will have sources for credible reference to build up your portfolio. You will also be training yourself for a much greater undertaking, more so, leadership. Such community helps you to hone your communication skills, interpersonal relationship skills, and much more importantly, leadership skills.

If you love sports and games, you can also create or join a sport or game team within your locality. It could be as simple as a jogging team, a scrabble team, a fitness team, darts team, dance team, martial arts team, table tennis team, etc. There will always be some people interested in such opportunities, only lacking initiative. You could be that initiative-in-waiting.

Network with your colleagues

If you are working remotely with others in the same company, then, it is good that you form a co-working group. If within the same locality, make an effort of meet physically. If not possible to meet physically, link up through platforms such as GoToMeeting, Slack or Skype. There are times when there is an overflow of work and a colleague can share with you extra work instead of turning it down. You too could find yourself being occasionally overwhelmed and thus need to share work with your colleagues. Sometimes, there are those projects that are huge and require an agency comprising of several workers. Being in touch with your colleagues can help you bid for such projects, which you alone could not undertake or qualify.

HOW TO GET YOUR FIRST PAID CLIENTS

Getting the first paid client is usually a breakthrough in your work-from-home venture. Many take painfully long time before hitting this breakthrough. Yet still, some others take quite a short time to hit this breakthrough and sustain a growth momentum. The difference rests in the approach made.

To help you make a quick breakthrough and sustain a growth momentum, we are going to look at ways and means of getting your first paid clients.

The following are some of the ways by which you can get your first paid clients:

1. Start at home

Charity begins at home. Let your family and loved ones know that you are venturing into work-from-home jobs. This way, they can help you spread the gospel and contribute to searching for potential leads. Spread your gospel to your friends and neighborhoods. Go further to your community organizations such as religious institutions, charity organizations, and other community groups. Participate in community events and let other participants know what you do. Yes, equip yourself with a job card to share out with those that you probably will not be able to engage in a detailed talk. The job card can talk on your behalf.

If you are a freelance writer, freelance graphic designer, or freelance event organizer, you will be surprised as to how your close contacts can create jobs for you. For example, as a freelance writer, some will want you to edit their CVs, resumes and even their profiles and portfolios. Some would want you to write business proposals for them and even help them draft various applications. If you are an academic writer, you are likely not to miss college and university students who would like you to assist them to prepare their essays, research papers, theses, dissertations, etc. If you happen to be a graphic designer, you will not miss some of them who would want you to design their custom cards, logos, decorations, etc. If you are an event organizer, you will not see some who would like you to organize their birthdays, weddings, anniversaries, children holiday parties, group celebrations, etc.

2. Start cold pitching

Cold pitching is about contacting potential clients and letting them know how you can help them grow their business. In this case, you can start-off by contacting startups, entrepreneurs, small businesses, and even bloggers. Many successful work-from-home entrepreneurs started this way. Sometimes, it is the best way to be assured of recurrent jobs as your clients appreciate your initiative.

To make cold pitching potentially successful, you need to:

- **Have an online presence** - More so, a blog of your own where you can provide more details about yourself. The good thing is that you do not have to incur the costs of hosting your own website. There are many free-host blog sites such as blogger.com and wordpress.org. All you need is to open a free account and start posting blogs. Post blogs relevant to your profession or task you endeavor to do. Make sure that potential clients can see a valuable solution on your blog.
- **Online portfolio** – An online portfolio is great. It helps you to show-off your achievements and accomplishments. Even if you are just a beginner with no project in your line of pursuit, show-off related projects. This could make potential clients appreciate your wider interests

While making your cold pitch, make sure that you incorporate the following:

- **How you found out about your potential clients** – If possible, a referee can be a great help.

- **Who you are** – Explain yourself in a manner that conveys the kind of personality for your type of undertaking
- **How you can serve them** – Point out potential areas where you can help your prospective clients. This means that you will need to do some background research on them.

3. Pitch to a Job Board Ad

Many job boards on the internet offer freelancing work. This is an opportunity for you to apply. This does well for freelance writers, freelance graphic designers, freelance coders, and such like projects.

The great thing about job boards is that you are not undercut through low-price bidding. When you qualify, you get what you deserve based on your competence rather than how cheap you are. Reputable companies, entrepreneurs, small businesses and even startups use job boards.

For a start, use free boards. This way, you do not risk much. The following are free job boards that can offer you a start:

- Contena

- Blogging Pro
- Problogger
- All Freelance Writing Job Board
- Canadian Freelance Writing (you can apply even if you are not a Canadian)

Freelancing sites with Job Boards include Upwork, Authentic Jobs, Smashing Jobs, Krop, and Fiverr. There are many more out there.

4. Get potential leads from Job Boards Tweets

Quite a number of job boards broadcast work-from-home jobs through Twitter. Following their Tweet handle can let you be aware of many opportunities to get a job.

The following are some of the more familiar Tweet handles:

- @twee-job
- @WahJobAgency
- @JJobs_tweets
- @Write_Jobs
- @WhoPaysWriters

5. Guest Post

There are good reputable sites where you can make a guest post. This you will do as a free assignment. However, you will reap much more than what you sacrificed by doing it without pay.

Reputable sites have thousands of visitors per day. This is a great way to expose yourself than paying for advertisement. On the other hand, guest posts help to build your portfolio and reference, of which ads cannot. If you are a starter and yet you do not have sufficient items to put into your portfolio, this is the best way to start.

6. Network with other colleagues in your sector

Find those who share your work-from-home mode of working and link up with them. You will not only get insights into how to find jobs but also get potential leads. Some of them could be having excess work. They can assign you some of it.

Networking events, social media, and professional organizations such as Freelancers Union and AIGA are some of the places where you can link up with like-minded work-from-home professionals. If you get in touch with those who have made success in this endeavor, simply ask them how they landed their first clients. They will be able to share with you their secrets, experiences, and tips that would greatly help you.

7. Join social platform groups

LinkedIn is a great platform for all types of professionals. Do not miss this out. LinkedIn has a job board. Just click on 'jobs' menu and it brings out a search bar for you to fill in the kind of job you are searching for.

Facebook Groups are also great for helping you find jobs. Join Facebook Groups related to your profession, skills, aspirations, and business. For example, the following are some of the groups that can be of benefit:

- The entrepreneur incubator
- The Smart Passive Income Community
- Online Entrepreneur Cash Generators

8. Warm pitching

Warm pitching is directly opposite of cold pitching. In warm pitching, you market yourself indirectly to potential clients by warming up to their hearts. You gradually build a relationship with them (brands and businesses). For example, follow them via their Twitter handle or like their Facebook page. Become a regular commentator with the aim of letting them notice you and thereby develop an engaging relationship. This way, you are in a better position to get their honest consideration as a known person rather than a stranger.

9. Hire Me!

It is always good to let people know that you are seeking a job. Most work-from-home candidates fear to do this. This is a great way to let your potential employers know that you are serious.

For example, in your portfolio, you can create a 'Hire Me!' button just after you have highlighted your work and at the end of it. You can also create a 'Hire Me!' button at the end of each blog post, linking to your contact form.

10.   Offer your free professional advice on an existing product/piece of work

You can offer advice in form of review, compliments, critique, etc. For example, if you are a web designer, you can offer a review of a company website by pointing out in areas that could improve user experience and even redesign it to prove your point. You can compliment a company's achievement in launching a product and offer yourself to be part of their continued success. You can also critique pieces of literature, performance, etc, if you are a professional in that field. Those who are this field greatly appreciate objective critique as it helps them improve on their weak areas. You could probably land some engagement into their future project. All these are geared towards proving your competence and availability for assignment.

11. Find out where your potential clients hang out

The best way to develop rapport and understanding of your potential clients is to hang out with them. For example:

- Content marketers/Writers – Scribophile, and Copyblogger forum are some of the online places you can find them.
- Designers – Designer News, Designer Chat, Reddit Web Design, and Sidebar are some of the places you can find designers for web products
- Coders and Programmers – Hacker News, Reddit Web Dev, and Hacker News Slack are some of the places programmers and coders hang around.

12. Collaborate

Successful work-from-home entrepreneurs usually have a lot of work and sometimes turn down others, more so, those that no longer pay them well. You can team up and collaborate with them so that they can assign you such jobs. Alternatively, they can subcontract you whenever they have extra work. Let them know that you are looking for such opportunity so that they do not feel that you are a competitor but co-worker/partner.

13. Do email marketing, video marketing, and paid advertisements

As a last option, you can choose paid advertisement for the job. However, before then, you can try email marketing by creating a short profile with a call to action message and emailing the same to your contacts. You can also create a YouTube video demonstrating what you do and market it (on your blog, portfolio, social media platforms and even email it).

MAINTAINING RELATIONSHIPS WITH YOUR CLIENTS

Business is about relationships. Without relationships, there is no work. The more relationships you create, the higher the chances of more business.

Maintaining relationships in work-from-home jobs is extremely critical. You even need it much more than you would need for an office setup. This is especially the case if you are an independent freelancer.

Why have good relationships?

Well, it is from relationships that we are born, nurtured, schooled and come of age as independent adults. We are social beings by nature. A relationship is a necessity to our survival just as air, water, and food. One cannot survive for long as a healthy human being without any form of relationship. In fact, a relationship is a yardstick of your health.

Good relationships with our colleagues make our work environment enjoyable. A good relationship with our loved ones at home and neighbors make a good home environment. It is out of cultivating a good relationship with our teachers in school and with our lecturers in colleges and universities that we build our careers. A good relationship with clients makes our business healthy, profitable and prosperous.

With good relationships, you are able to be free and creative. You are not worried about enemies or those who wish you ill. With good relationships, you do not see problems but challenging opportunities. This is a great attitude that you need to succeed in your work-from-home career.

What makes a good relationship?

Well, just as having a balanced diet requires great ingredients, so is a relationship. The following are the critical ingredients of a well-balanced relationship:

- **Mindfulness** – This refers to being consciously aware of your thoughts, words, and deeds. More so, being aware of their impact on others.
- **Trust** – This refers to being able to have faith in others honesty and ability to honor their commitments.
- **Mutual Respect** – This refers to holding each other in high esteem. Thus, you value each other's opinion, perspective, effort, and input. You deliberately seek not to

dominate others but work together towards achieving set goals.

- **Openness** – This refers to an attitude that allows you to be free from fear, suspicions, and worries about how others take your thoughts, words, and actions. It is being free to express yourself without reservations. Openness thrives in a climate of trust and mutual respect. It is in such an environment that you know that even if you are wrong, you will be understood and be corrected without your respect being compromised.

- **Love for diversity** – It is almost inevitable that when you work from home, more so, in a global environment, that you will interact with people from diverse backgrounds. Each of these backgrounds has its own cultural filters such that things are bound to be interpreted differently from one cultural background to another. Sometimes you may make an innocent joke, which in your culture will cause laughter and lively talk, but in some other cultures, it may be interpreted as rude, obscene or in bad taste. Learning other people's culture and appreciating their worldviews will greatly help you to cope with such situations.

How to Build Good Work Relationships with your clients

Building good work relationships with your clients require deliberate effort. You just do not assume that it will happen naturally on its own. You have to work towards it.

The following are key things that you need to do:

1. **Develop Your People Skills**

   A good relationship requires people skills. You need good people skills to be able to cultivate this relationship. These 'soft skills' include communication, collaboration, and conflict resolution. To establish your people skills level, take a soft skills test – there are several soft skills tests online, which you can take to establish your level of competency in them. Simply type "soft skills test" in your Google Search Bar and several will come up. These tests will help you identify your weaknesses and thus be able to address them appropriately.

2. **Identify your relationship needs**

   What are you looking for in your relationship with your client? Do you know the kind of relationship the clients are looking for you? By understanding your relationship needs and those of your clients, you can successfully build stronger and productive relationships with them.

3. Schedule time to build relationships

Building relationships is as important to your work as any other activity. Thus, give it the same priority you would give any other client assignment. Devote regular time towards relationship building. It can be even just half an hour, broken down into 5-minute portions and spread out during the day. You can take this time to call someone, even a past client or a colleague. You can get into your LinkedIn group and post or reply to comments. You can use Twitter handle or Facebook to share out some idea or content. The focus should be on people related to your work.

4. Focus on Your Emotional Intelligence (EI)

Work on your Emotional Intelligence so that you can be in harmony with your clients. EI refers to your ability to recognize emotions, understand them and channel them towards a productive purpose.

EI is the cement that glues together strong relationships.

5. Be optimistic

Express optimism in your undertaking. Whenever a client gives you work, do not express pessimism. Pessimism could be the trigger that can make him change his mind and withdraw the project. Even your client needs positive affirmation from you. Sometimes the client may be having some reservations and self-doubt. Your optimism will clear this self-doubt while your pessimism will embolden them making the client probably shelve the project. It is good to be optimistic for it is not just for your sake but also for your client's sake. Optimism on your part will build client's confidence in you and your abilities and thus result in further assignments in future and more likely, a recommendation to his friends and partners. This will undoubtedly expand your network.

6. Manage boundaries

Everyone needs private space. Even if your relationship with your client gets personal, still, manage boundaries to stay professional. This way, you will keep each other from trespassing into another's private space. Trespassing into someone's private space negates good relationship.

7. Keep off gossiping

Do not gossip about your client, no matter who you are talking to. You never know how this can pan out. Gossips have a way of spreading out and reaching the targeted victim in unexpected ways. Furthermore, gossiping corrupts your mindset and attitude towards your client. It reinforces your negative patterns in the mind. This eventually weakens and kills an otherwise good relationship.

8. **Smoothen out difficult relationships**

   Conflicts do happen in any relationship that there is, your relationship with your client not being an exception. Conflicts are due to different perspectives or different expectations. Conflicts are healthy. It is all about how you go about managing them. Use your soft skills to iron them. Your client will come to senses and greatly appreciate you.

How to make clients appreciate your professional undertaking:

- **Get to know your clients** – It is important to know your clients. Studying their profile, contacting their previous employees, going through their previous assignments and having an interview with them are just but some of the ways by which you can learn about your clients. Sometimes you may find out that you are not compatible with your potential client. It would be better to avoid further engagement than disappoint each other later on, with serious repercussions to your very own reputation. Having a small talk with clients can help in shaping your understanding of them. They too can have a better understanding of you.

- **Share testimonials and work samples** – Your previous work tells you a lot about how you perform. This can help your clients manage their expectations of you.

- **Email like a professional** – The way you present your communication with your client can easily tell whether you are professional in your undertakings or not. It is not so much about being formal (though necessary) but more about being relevant, clear and concise. Converse with your client as you would with a colleague. Present a warm, friendly tone yet not too casual. Whenever you have a phone conversation, be sure to make a follow-up with an email outlining key points discussed so that both of you can be on the same level of understanding.

- **Be respectful of their time** – Keep in mind that both you and your client are busy. Stay on schedule. Respect appointments. Be on time. If you are unable to make it and thus must reschedule the meeting, inform your client soonest possible.

- **Do not flake from jobs** – Sometimes, it happens that, due to unavoidable circumstances, you are not able to take up the job or continue it. The worst thing is to abscond. You not only break the relationship but also trust with future clients. It is better to communicate with the client and offer better alternatives. If you took up the job and it is too much, or for some reason, it is not your type of job, smoothen out the transition. Do the bit that you can and recommend to client other persons who can help out, or substitute you.

- **Meet your commitments** – Meet your side of commitment. If it is an agreed deadline, keep it. If for some reasons, you are unable to meet the deadline, promptly request for an extension while providing adequate reasons for the same.

- **Communicate effectively** – Express yourself clearly and confirm that you have been understood. Listen keenly to your client and be confident to ask questions where you feel that you have not gotten the instructions clearly.

- **Be honest and transparent** – Honesty pays, at least in the end. In case you make a mistake, do honestly explain how it happened and genuinely apologize. Explain how you are going to remedy it and be ready to affirm that you are going to avoid it in future. Above all, be honest about your skills, level of knowledge and capabilities.

- **Request for feedback** – It is important to know what clients feel about what you have done. This way, you can strengthen the positive aspects and improve on the weaker aspects. The client will be willing to be more patient with you if you request honest feedback and be willing to take it positively however adverse it may seem to be. Every feedback is an opportunity to learn and grow in your profession. It is also an opportunity for your client to have trust in you and thus invest more in you. This proves to your client that you value his/her opinion and you are ready to learn and grow. This makes you client have confidence in your professionalism, and be willing to expand the scope of your work in future.

- **Be who you are** – Be genuine. Do not fear your client noticing your weaknesses. Turn your weaknesses into understandable strengths. Clients will be more willing to be patient with you if they understand and appreciate your weaknesses than if they do not. They will be more trusting and help you to mitigate or overcome those weaknesses. Trust does not come easily. However, it is the most valuable thing that clients cannot easily get and substitute. Thus, when they trust you, they are more willing to forego certain aspects in order to gain more.

- **Go the extra mile** – Always endeavor to improve your work. This cultivates the spirit of excellence in you. Do not do shoddy work because the pay is low. This will eventually hurt you, as it becomes your habit of underperformance. Strive to excel no matter the pay.

- **Be empathetic** – Always put yourself in your client's shoes. This way, you can understand where it pinches them. You will be able to understand the impact of your actions or inactions on their wellbeing. They too have businesses and any action or inaction on your part affects their business. Work towards taking action that prevent or remedy adverse effects on their side.

Tips to keep clients comfortably engaged

1. Smile – Many people mistakenly assume that you need not have a smile while communicating remotely. A smile has an effect on the tone of your voice. People will feel it even if they do not see it. Radiate a smile on your cheeks, in your eyes, voice, and heart. These will warm-up your client and ease out communication. Even if you are drafting an email, a smile will help you naturally find warm words to express your joy.

2. Make eye contact – More often than not, a client will request a video conversation. When you are engaging in video calls, for example, over Skype, Hangout or Facebook Messenger, make sure that you look at your client openly, warmly and direct in the eye.

3. Open your body language – Whether you are engaging in a video call or not, open up your body language. This has an effect on how you express yourself - more so when you are in a tense conversation with a client. This helps to release tension. To open up - open your chest, your heart and your arms.

4. Address your client by name – Using a client's name while addressing him/her helps to build rapport. It also shows keenness to be friendly. It is also a sign of respect. Call them by their names while greeting them, when asking a question, when giving them thanks, and when bidding them farewell.

5. Speak in a formal yet friendly tone – Warm your tone and tamper it with kindness and love.

6. Be present – Whenever you are conversing with a client, avoid distractions such as attending to some other people or tasks. Give full attention to the client. This will help you avoid an embarrassing scenario where you are forced to request a client to repeat the question or assuming the question and answering it wrong. Being present is part of being self-aware.

7. Express gratitude – Everyone loves to feel appreciated. Gratitude brings a sense of emotional connection. See and express goodness in others. Be frank and open with your appreciation and give thanks. More importantly, be genuine. Gratitude is an attitude that you can cultivate through positive thinking. Another way to express gratitude is by being generous. Give back to your client. You can give back by sharing knowledge that is not ordinarily dispensed in the course of your work. This could be in form of eBooks, manuals or magazines or simply general advice or suggestions.

8. Take necessary breaks – While conversing, it is important to slow down. Breathe slowly and deeply as you give your client a chance to respond to you. This not only helps to relieve tension but also helps to ventilate your mind for a more productive engagement.

9. Manifest empathy and compassion – There are those occasions when your client could be in a bad situation – for example, loss of an important contract or bid, loss of a loved one, or some other unfortunate event. Having built a strong relationship, you will not assume that this is none of your business concern. You need to express empathy and compassion towards them. This is the best way to honor their emotional experiences. Validate and

appreciate their feelings so that they feel heard, understood and appreciated.

10. Manifest integrity – Integrity is about living and conducting yourself according to your values. Let your thoughts, words and deeds match. Promise what you have the will and ability to deliver.

11. Nurture good manners – Manners have a way of showing themselves in unexpected ways. Nurture good manners so that in whatever the situation, only they can possibly come out. Above all, be courteous, polite and gracious.

12. Demonstrate thought leadership – Whatever you are doing on behalf of your client, it is a product of your thoughts. Demonstrate thought leadership by being able to guide your client where needed. You are a professional in your respective field. Do not restrain yourself from giving your thoughts, and more so, on how a given task can be performed better and more productively.

13. Express genuine compliments – There are times when a client goes the extra mile just to ensure that you are able to do your job the best way possible. Do not withhold your compliments. Express them honestly. Do not force

yourself to compliment when it is not out of your heart. Let it be, only from your heart.

14. Practice good habits – Some of the good habits that can foster a strong and lasting relationship include courtesy, politeness, truthfulness, patience, reliability, taking responsibility and giving salutations.

15. Be forgiving and apologetic – Whatever the case, we must not forget that we are human beings, not robots. Thus, making mistakes is part of our human nature, no matter how much we do our best to avoid them. When your client makes mistakes, do not take it lightly. Be forgiving. This will raise the standard so that your client may find the abundance to forgive you too. When you make mistake, do apologize. Sometimes, even when you feel no wrongdoing on your part but the client feels slighted, do apologize. This way, the client will appreciate that you recognize his/her feelings.

CONCLUSION

Thank you for developing a keen interest in this book to the point of acquiring it to read. I further thank you for taking your time and effort to read it through to the end.

It is my sincere hope that you have gained valuable information from this book and that you have been inspired to find your own work-from-home jobs or businesses. It is also my sincere hope that you have been able to share with others information about this book so that they can have a copy of it as their work-from-home companion.

Again, thank you for acquiring and reading this book.

Have a good luck!

www.ingramcontent.com/pod-product-compliance
Lightning Source LLC
Chambersburg PA
CBHW071509210326
41597CB00018B/2706